BLACK'S JUNIOR REFERENCE BOOKS

General Editor: R. J. Unstead

1	A HISTORY OF HOUSES	R. J. Unstead
2	DEEP SEA FISHING	John. M. Wright
3	TRAVEL BY ROAD	R. J. Unstead
4	THE STORY OF AIRCRAFT	Robert J. Hoare
5	LIFE BEFORE MAN	Duncan Forbes
6	COAL MINING	John Davey
7	THE STORY OF THE THEATRE	David Male
8	STARS AND SPACE	Patrick Moore
9	MONASTERIES	R. J. Unstead
10	TRAVEL BY SEA	Robert J. Hoare
11	FURNITURE	Frank Turland
12	MUSICAL INSTRUMENTS	Denys Darlow
13	ARMS AND ARMOUR	Frederick Wilkinson
14	FARMING	Frank Huggett
15	LAW AND ORDER	John Dumpleton
16	BRITISH RAILWAYS TODAY	P. Ransome-Wallis
17	HERALDRY	Rosemary Manning
18	COSTUME	Phillis Cunnington
19	THE STORY OF THE POST	Robert Page
20	MAN IN SPACE	Henry Brinton
21	CASTLES	R. J. Unstead

FIRST EDITION 1963; SECOND EDITION 1970
ISBN 0 7136 1079 4

PUBLISHED BY A. AND C. BLACK LTD
4, 5 AND 6 SOHO SQUARE LONDON W1V 6AD

MADE IN GREAT BRITAIN
PRINTED BY MORRISON AND GIBB LTD, LONDON AND EDINBURGH

CONTENTS

ACKNOWLEDGEMENTS

Grateful acknowledgement is made to the following for permission to reproduce photographs, prints and engravings: British Museum, pages 15(c), 21(b), 30(a), 37(b), 38(a), 41(a and b), 42(a and b), 43(b), 45(a), 49(a), 52(a), 64(a); Central Office of Information: Crown Copyright, page 74(a); City of Bradford Police, page 77(a); City of London Police, page 71(a), 75(b), 77(b); Corpus Christi College, Cambridge, page 10(a); Devon and Cornwall Constabulary, pages 71(b and c), 77(c), 78(a); London Museum, pages 5(b), 33, 35(c), 36(a), 51(b), 53(a); Mansell Collection, pages 36(b), 37(a), 45(b), 50(a and b), 57(d), 59, 60(a), 64(b), 75(a); National Buildings Record, pages 31(a), 62(a); National Portrait Gallery, pages 46, 51(a), 54(a), 56(a), 61(b and c); New Scotland Yard, pages 62(b), 72, 73(c), 74(b), 76(a and b), 77(d), 78(b); Radio Times Hulton Picture Library, pages 35(a and b), 38(b), 39(a), 58(b), 66(a); F. Wilkinson, pages 60(b, c and d), 66(b).

The drawing on page 5(c) is from *Ancient Greek, Roman and Byzantine Costume* by Mary Houston; those on pages 14(a), 18(d), 22(a), 26(c and d), 28(b), 30(d), 40(a), 42(a and b), 67(b) are from *Mediaeval London*, *London in the Time of the Tudors and Stuarts*, and *London in the Nineteenth Century*, by Sir Walter Besant; on pages 9(a, b, c and d), 11(c) from *English Costume of the Early Middle Ages* by Iris Brooke; on pages 22(c), 25(b and c) from *English Costume in the Elizabethan Age* by Iris Brooke; on pages 16(a), 19(b) from *English Costume in the Later Middle Ages* by Iris Brooke; on pages 14(c), 20(a) from *Mediaeval Costume in England and France* by Mary Houston.

The cover illustrations are reproduced by kind permission of the Daily Telegraph Colour Library (front cover) and the Devon and Cornwall Constabulary (back cover).

1. HOW MEN KEPT THE LAW IN OLDEN TIMES

From earliest times, ever since men began to live in family groups, they had to behave according to the customs of the tribe. The chief and the elders made sure that everybody obeyed these tribal laws, and banishment from the tribe was probably the most severe punishment for a wrongdoer.

The worst punishment for early man was banishment from his tribe

THE ROMANS RULE BRITAIN

When the Romans conquered Britain, they brought their own system of law. Because they had plenty of highly-trained soldiers who were well disciplined, the Romans were able to make the conquered peoples obey their laws.

As soon as the military commanders had the country under control, the Romans began building towns. These were usually governed by magistrates, who were chosen by the citizens of the town.

Roman London was governed by magistrates

A Roman soldier

In Verulamium, for instance, when Alban was arrested for sheltering a runaway Christian, he was sentenced to death by the Roman magistrate, who was carrying out the decree of his Emperor. The 'police' who arrested Alban and carried out the sentence were soldiers.

Roman soldiers arrest St. Alban

Saxon raiders laid waste towns, and the Roman laws were soon forgotten

LAWLESS TIMES

Eventually the Roman armies had to leave Britain, after having been here for four hundred years. The people left behind were defenceless against the ferocious Saxon warriors who sailed across the North Sea, at first to raid, and then to settle in a land more fertile than their own.

The towns were laid waste and the Roman system of law and order, known as the 'Pax Romana', or Peace of the Romans, quickly disappeared. Justice, trade and peaceful life were almost forgotten.

The Saxons destroy London in A.D. *530*

SAXON LAW AND ORDER

The Saxons liked to live in small communities, and did not build towns as the Romans did. As the invaders settled down to village life, a rough and ready system of justice developed to protect lives and property.

The Saxons lived in small communities, not in towns

'Manslaying', wounding and cattle-stealing were common crimes in those times.

Whatever the crime, the rest of the village turned against the offender, and he was seized and dragged before the Folk Moot.

Pig-stealing was a common crime

The Moot was a meeting, held in the open, attended by all the older men of the village. Each family chose one of its menfolk to speak and act for it at the Folk Moot. There were no special judges, such as the Romans had.

If it was decided, after hearing both the man who was accused and the person he had wronged, that the accused was guilty, he was either hanged straight away or made to pay a fine. Sometimes he was punished by being made a slave or by having a hand chopped off.

An offender before the Folk Moot

CHRISTIANITY COMES TO ENGLAND

When the Christian Church in Rome sent missionaries to southern England to convert the heathen Saxons, the teachings of Jesus began to affect the way in which people lived. They became more peace-loving, and kinder towards each other.

Missionaries were sent to preach to the Saxons

The Christian missionaries not only brought a better way of life, but they also brought the art of writing.

At last, the laws of the Saxons, which had been handed down by word of mouth for hundreds of years, could be recorded in writing.

In about the year 700, Ine, King of Wessex, sent men round the countryside to find out the best of the old customs, and then he had all the laws written down in a large book which was called ‘The Dooms of Ine’. (A ‘doom’ was a law, or a judgement.)

A monk writes down the laws

Ine's men collecting information

THE LAWS OF KING ALFRED

A century and a half later, Wessex had another king. His name was Alfred. Alfred was very interested in books and learning, and he decided to rewrite Ine's laws.

King Alfred revised Ine's laws

At the beginning of his book he wrote :

> ' That which you do not wish other men to do to you, do ye not to them. From this one doom a man may decide how he should judge everyone rightly. He needs no other doom book.'

Alfred's laws included very detailed instructions of punishments for various wrongs. Most of these punishments were fines. If a man could not, or would not, pay a fine he was made a thrall or slave.

The wergild or man-price of a nobleman was six times that of a churl

In those days, every man had a money value, according to his importance. This was called ' wergild ', or ' man-price '. A nobleman was worth about six times as much as an ordinary freeman, who was called a churl.

A thrall had no wergild

The wergild of a churl was very little

If a man was killed, deliberately or accidentally, his relatives were entitled to his wergild. This had to be paid by the killer or by his family, and it ended the matter. The great value of the wergild was that it stopped family blood-feuds.

Wounding, too, was a common crime in Alfred's time, and the fine varied according to the severity of the wound. For example:

> ' If a man's arm with the hand be entirely cut off before the elbow, let the fine be eighty shillings.'

The value of a thumb cut off was thirty shillings, but if only the nail had been removed, the fine was five shillings. 'If the shooting finger be struck off, let the fine be eight shillings.'

Gyf ðe ðuma bið of aslagen ðam sceall
ðrittig. scill to bote. Gyf se nægel bið of
aslagen seo bot bið fif . . scill. Gyf se scy-
te finger bið of aslagen. seo bot bið fifty-
ne. scill. his nægles beoð. iiii. scill. Gyf
se midlesta finger sy of aslagen. seo bot
bið. xii. scill. his nægles. ii. scill. Gyf se
gold finger sy of aslægen. to ðam sculon
seofentyne. scill to bote. his nægles. iiii.

This part of King Alfred's laws begins: 'If the thumb is struck off, thirty shillings must be paid as compensation for it. If the nail is struck off, five shillings must be paid as compensation'

Wrongdoers in Saxon times were never punished by being sent to prison, because there were no prisons. The punishment of death was kept for the most serious crimes, which were called 'bootless' crimes ('bootless' means 'without compensation'). These crimes could not be paid for by fines. They included obvious murder, housebreaking, open theft, and treachery to one's lord.

King Alfred did his best to make sure that his laws were properly kept and that the courts were fair.

The good order that the king expected in his kingdom was called the King's Peace. Anyone who committed a crime broke the Peace, and by doing so wronged the king.

In Saxon times there were no police, so there was always the problem of making sure that the criminal would come to court to be tried. Therefore his family was punished if he did not appear, or refused to pay the fine.

Some bootless crimes, which were punishable by death

If the family did not produce the accused man, he was declared an outlaw. From then on, he was said to bear the 'wolf's head'. This meant that anyone could kill him on sight as if he were a wolf.

A man declared an outlaw had to hide, for he could be killed on sight

The lord had to make sure that his man came to court for trial

Under King Athelstan, who was Alfred's grandson, a law was made ordering every man to have a lord. Then the lord was made responsible for seeing that his man came to court for trial.

HUNDRED AND SHIRE MOOTS

Athelstan also arranged that the land should be divided into districts called 'Hundreds'. Each Hundred had a court which met once every four weeks. Above this there was a Shire Moot, which met twice or three times a year.

An Ealdorman with his servant

In north-east England, which was occupied by the Danes, the Hundreds were known as 'Wapentakes'.

The head man at the Hundred Moot was the king's reeve. He was a man chosen by the king to see that the royal orders were carried out in the Hundred.

The Shire Moot was in charge of an ealdorman. He was a noble who governed the county, or sometimes a much larger district, for the king. Later on, the ealdormen were called earls. If the ealdorman was absent, the Shire Moot was presided over by the shire reeve (sheriff).

The Shire Moot was held two or three times a year

When a man appeared before a court to answer the charge, he was usually allowed to swear an oath that he was innocent. He would do this with the aid of 'oath-helpers'.

Oath-helpers were respectable friends of the accused man, and each swore that the man's own oath was honest. They swore :

> 'By the Lord, the oath is pure and not false which this man swore.'

The number of oath-helpers needed depended on the seriousness of the charge. If a man had enough friends to swear that they believed him innocent, he usually went free.

If, however, a man was a suspicious character who had frequently been accused, he was no longer 'oath-worthy'. That is, his oath was of no value.

In such a case, a person who had been wronged could bring forward *his* oath-helpers to swear to the wrong-doer's guilt.

If there were witnesses of the crime, they would swear against the accused man in this manner :

> 'In the name of Almighty God, so I stand here by Wulfric in true witness, unbidden and unbought, as I saw with my eyes and heard with my ears that which I pronounce with him.'

In early times the folk-moots were held in the open air, usually under a sacred or venerable tree, by a large stone, or on a prominent hill. Many of these landmarks had probably been meeting places for hundreds of years. They often gave their names to the district. Maidstone, Kent, Appletree, Derbyshire, and Spelhoe ('hill of speech'), Northamptonshire, are such places.

TRIAL BY ORDEAL

When a wrong-doer could not bring forward enough oath-helpers, the accused man might then have to go to the Ordeal, the judgement of God.

Ordeal by fire

There was, for example, Ordeal by Fire, which took place in church before a priest. The accused man had to carry a piece of red-hot iron in his bare hand while he walked three paces. Then his hand was bandaged by a priest. If, at the end of three days, it was healing properly, it was taken as a sign from God that the man was innocent. But if the hand was festering, he was guilty.

Ordeal by water (1)

In Ordeal by Water, a man had to plunge his hand into a cauldron of boiling water and take out a stone.

Ordeal by water (2)

In another form of Ordeal by Water, the accused was thrown into a pond or river. If he sank, he was innocent, and was immediately rescued. On the other hand, if he floated, he was guilty.

Ordeal by morsel

The least unpleasant ordeal, which was used for members of the clergy, was called Ordeal by Morcel. A piece of bread was put into the accused's mouth, in the belief that it would choke him if he were guilty. If he were innocent, he would have no difficulty in swallowing it.

2. KEEPING THE LAW IN THE MIDDLE AGES

William the Conqueror (from the Bayeux Tapestry)

The tithing chooses a tithingman

When William, Duke of Normandy, conquered England he made few changes in the Saxon system of law and order, though he made sure that the laws were strictly kept.

FRANKPLEDGE

William enforced the old system of dividing each town or village into ' tithings ', or groups of ten men. These ten were responsible for each other, and they chose one of the group to represent them at the local courts. This man was known as the ' tithingman ', or chief pledge.

Knights, servants, women and girls were not members of a tithing

Every villein above the age of twelve, who was not a household servant, had to be ' in pledge ', that is, a member of a tithing. Thus, a man had nine others to make sure that he behaved himself, for if he committed a crime or ran away, they were punished for his fault.

The only people who were permitted to remain outside the Frankpledge, apart from servants, were boys under twelve, women and girls, priests, knights and barons.

Special courts were held twice a year in each township to see that the rules about Frankpledge were carried out. Such a court was called a ' View of Frankpledge '.

A Court Leet, at which cases of wrong-doing were reported

Each tithingman was bound to report the misdoings of his own group, and was fined if he did not. Cases of wrong-doing were usually reported, or ' presented ', at the Court Leet. This was a court held by the Lord of the Manor to deal with crime.

In Norwich, then one of the greatest cities in the land, the Court Leet Rolls for 1288 record that :

> ' The chief pledges . . . present on their oath that Ernald de Castro wounded Hugh de Bromholm and drew blood from him contrary to the peace.'

The offences presented at the Courts Leet were very numerous, and even included murder and manslaughter, although such serious crimes had to be passed on to one of the king's courts. The main presentments were for small thefts, assaults, raising the hue and cry wrongfully, nuisances of all sorts and market and trade offences.

A tradesman who sold bad goods was dragged round the town with the goods round his neck

Serious crimes were tried and punished by a King's Court

THE CONSTABLE

Each year a local man was elected by his neighbours at the Court Leet to be Constable for the next twelve months. He was given a staff, which was his badge of office.

The constable was not a full-time paid officer as he is now, but he had to do the job without reward, as well as doing his ordinary work.

These are some of the duties of the constable :

1. *To keep a strict watch at all times.*
If need be, the constable had to find watchmen to help him do this and he was expected to see that they were watchful and alert when on duty.

2. *To take charge of any wrongdoer handed over to him.*
Anyone who found a person committing a crime was supposed to arrest him. The constable had to take charge of the prisoner and keep him safely until he could be brought to trial.

3. *To follow with the hue and cry.*
If a wrongdoer was chased, the constable had to drop anything he was doing and join in the chase.

Investigating a brawl

The constable and a watchman take a thief into custody

4. *To inquire into offences.*
If a crime had been committed, the constable was expected to try and find out who had done it.

5. *To report all crimes.*
The constable had to report to the courts of law 'all blood-sheddings, affrays, outcries, rescues (of prisoners), and other offences committed or done against the King's peace'.

6. *To serve warrants and summons.*
He had to see that offenders were brought to justice. A warrant was a written order to the constable from a court, telling him to take some particular action, such as arresting a certain person. A summons was an order to the offender to attend his trial.

7. *To obey all the lawful commands of the High Constable and the courts.*
In many districts there was a more important constable called the High Constable, who had to see that the other constables did their jobs properly.

HUE AND CRY

If a man was seen to steal, and he then ran off, the cry was immediately raised. On hearing the shouts of 'Out ! Out !' all able-bodied men and youths left their work and rushed pell-mell to follow the chase.

It was the duty of the constable to rouse the parish to help him pursue the wrongdoer, and in early days he sounded the alarm on a horn. The sound of this was the 'hue', and the shouts of alarm were the 'cry'.

If the criminal escaped across the parish boundary, the constable had to rouse the constable of the next parish, so that the hue and cry could be continued. Any parish which did not do its duty, and thus allowed the wrongdoer to escape, not only had to pay a fine to the king, but also had to repay the person who had been robbed or injured.

People were frequently taken to court for failing in their duty. At Wilton a woman was imprisoned for failing to raise the alarm when one of her neighbours murdered a certain Richard, a stranger.

In the few large towns, like London, it was more difficult to pursue the hue and cry. Their narrow, crooked and unlighted ways gave fleeing criminals a good chance of escape. Nevertheless, six young men who attacked the London Watch one June night in 1302 were quickly captured. The records of the Lord Mayor's Court tell us that the assault took place as midnight was striking at St. Paul's. The six men made off, but the hue and cry was raised 'by horn and voice' and men from the neighbouring wards had run to help.

When they heard the shouts of 'Out ! Out !' all the men in the village left their work and rushed to follow the chase. This hue and cry is chasing a man who has stolen a pig.

A criminal seeks sanctuary at the porch of a church

An abjurer setting out from the sanctuary

SANCTUARY

Sometimes a criminal who was on the run would seek 'sanctuary'. If he could reach the porch of a church, or the house of a priest, before his pursuers caught up with him, he could claim the protection of God. No one, except a priest, was allowed to touch a man in sanctuary.

If a thief or burglar took sanctuary he had to hand back the goods which he had stolen. He could then choose to do one of two things: he could surrender to the King's Peace, that is, give himself up to justice; or he could 'abjure the realm'.

A sanctuary door-knocker

An abjurer had to walk into the sea up to his knees

A man who abjured the realm agreed to leave the country and not return.

While he was making up his mind what he intended to do, his pursuers kept a careful watch outside. If he tried to escape they would take him at once.

A wrongdoer who abjured the realm had to appear from time to time at the door of the church, to admit his guilt and to swear to leave England for ever.

Eventually, he had to set off 'un-girt, unshod, bareheaded, in his bare shirt, as if he were to be hanged on the gallows, having received a cross in his hands'.

When he reached the port, he was bound to walk out into the sea up to his knees, to show his willingness to leave the country.

WATCH AND WARD

The watch at the gate question a stranger

The gates of walled towns had to be shut between sunset and sunrise. A law passed in 1285 ordered every city to station a watch of six men at each gate. Strangers were not allowed to pass the gates during the hours of darkness. Any who tried to do so were arrested by the watch. If in the morning the watch found any cause for suspicion, they had to hand the strangers over to the sheriff.

Members of a Peace Guild

In London, and a few other towns, the more important citizens banded themselves into Peace Guilds. All the members were divided into groups of ten, and paid fourpence each into a common fund. If any member had goods or money stolen, his loss was made good from this fund. The Peace Guilds conducted their business at a folk moot which was held three times a year. This moot could outlaw offenders, who were then branded, and driven out of the city.

THE KING'S JUDGES

King Henry II arranged that his judges, instead of sitting at Westminster, should travel regularly round the country. This was to make sure that all people accused of serious crimes received a fair and speedy trial.

Royal judges travelling to the assizes

The royal judges held courts in the important towns to deal with the most serious crimes. These courts became known as the Assizes, from a French word ' assise ' which meant ' sitting '.

TWELVE GOOD MEN AND TRUE

Henry also provided that the royal judges should be assisted by juries. It was an ancient custom to call together a group of local men to assist in finding out true facts. A jury was made up of ' twelve good men and true ' who had to swear an oath to declare the truth, whatever the truth might be.

Thus, in time, it came about that juries, after listening carefully to all the evidence, had to say whether a man was guilty or not. The judge was obliged to accept the opinion of the jury.

King John

Not all kings cared for making and keeping good laws. King John was forced by the barons to seal an agreement to behave more justly. This was called Magna Carta : the Great Charter.

The court of King's Bench (At the top are five judges ; below them are the clerks ; on the left is the jury and in the centre the prisoner. In front other prisoners in fetters are awaiting trial)

JUSTICES OF THE PEACE

In the countryside the landowners were expected to see that the law was enforced and the less important criminals punished.

These country gentleman, who gave their time without pay to help maintain the King's Peace, became known as Justices of the Peace. At the Shire Court it was their duty to assist the Sheriff, who was the king's representative in the county.

Justices of the Peace were chosen by the king, and Edward III ordained that no man should ' go offensively ' or ' ride armed ' before the justices. In each county, the justices met four times a year to transact their business. These quarterly meetings became known as Quarter Sessions.

THE BARONS DEFY THE LAW

During the Middle Ages, powerful barons often ignored the laws of the land, and managed to bribe or frighten judges into giving false judgements.

Under a weak or youthful king, and especially during the Wars of the Roses, the barons and their lawless followers terrorised the countryside.

Rogues and outlaws became retainers of evil lords, and thus were able to wear the lord's livery, or uniform. When they were not fighting for the baron, they often roamed the countryside in fierce gangs, doing all sorts of evil.

On one occasion the Duke of Norfolk seized Caister Castle by surrounding it with 3000 men-at-arms. He had so many men in his pay that he could afford to ignore the King's Peace.

Soldiers pillaging a house

Judges were often bribed by wealthy men

A letter written by one of the Paston family of Norfolk, during the fifteenth century, tells us :

> 'They ride about the country, and take sheep and cattle where they will ; they pull men out of their houses, and kill or beat them ; they waylay men on the high road ; they even entered the chancel of Hasingham Church and there attacked the parson ; they molest and beat old women ; and so terrorise the countryside that people for fear of murder dare not abide in their houses, nor ride, nor walk about their occupations without protection.'

Retainers, wearing the lord's livery, roamed the countryside in fierce gangs

3. LAW AND ORDER IN TUDOR AND STUART TIMES

During the Wars of the Roses, most of the barons took one side or the other, but at the end of more than thirty years' bitter fighting their power and wealth was broken. Many great lords had died in battle or had been executed by their victorious enemies.

King Henry VII

The Battle of Bosworth ended the Wars of the Roses which broke the wealth and power of the barons

Henry Tudor was crowned king, as Henry VII. He was a firm and clever man who made up his mind to restore law and order to the kingdom.

The people of the middle class made sure that Henry's new laws were kept

One of the first things that Henry did was to get a law passed forbidding the nobles to keep retainers. Because he was unwilling to allow the nobles much power, the King depended on the middle class of well-to-do citizens—country gentlemen, lawyers, and merchants—to see that the laws were kept.

Country gentlemen were chosen to act as Justices of the Peace. The King made sure that they did their job thoroughly. For instance, he ordered them to see that beggars and vagabonds were dealt with more severely.

A beggar in the stocks

This old map shows the sanctuary of St. Martin's the Grand. It was the largest and the safest of all the English sanctuaries. The map shows the church, the window, and the two posts which mark the corners of the sanctuary

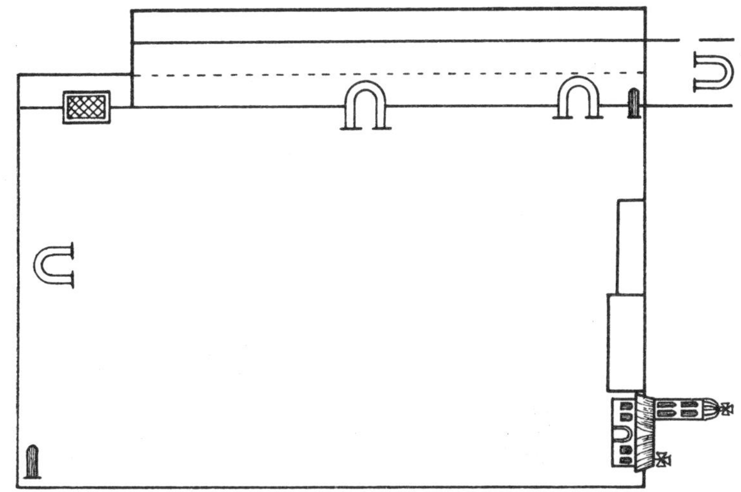

Henry VII discovered that many people were escaping proper punishment by claiming 'Benefit of Clergy'. If, after committing a murder or a robbery, a man could prove that he could read a few verses from the Bible, he was tried, not by the King's judges, but in a Church Court. These courts were much less strict, so the man would probably get off with a light punishment.

The Church had had its own courts since the time of William the Conqueror. Now times were changing, and Henry VII ordered that guilty clergymen should be branded on the hands. Murderers, for example, were to be marked with an M.

In large towns like London, the right of sanctuary had become a nuisance. Not only could criminals seek sanctuary at church doors, but they claimed sanctuary on any property belonging to the Church.

Some of these places covered quite a lot of ground, and many escaping rogues made their homes there, safe from capture.

In the country, things were different. One writer tells us that there 'every unknown face was challenged and examined'. If strangers could not give a good account of themselves they were taken before the Justice.

The Justice questions two suspects

ROGUES AND VAGABONDS

In Tudor times, the country was pestered by a large increase in the numbers of sturdy beggars and vagabonds.

Some were men-at-arms, retainers and serving-men turned adrift now that the Wars of the Roses were over. Some had been servants at the monasteries closed by Henry VIII, and others were labourers and cottagers who had lost their work and their strips of land when some great man enclosed the fields for sheep.

The old ways of life on the manor were changing. For centuries, men had worked for their lord, and in return, he had protected them. When all men were tied to the land, unemployment was hardly known. But now that men began to work for wages, a bad harvest, a hard landlord or a fall in the wool trade put men out of work and out of home too.

Poor people were often driven to crime

Nicholas Jennings, a notorious rogue of the time, often wore disguise so that he would not be recognised. This old drawing shows him disguised as a sailor, and calling himself Nicholas Blunt (left), and as a beggar (right)

There was little or no help for the unlucky ones, for the cripples, the blind and the idiots. They kept themselves from starving by begging, or they grew desperate and joined the bands of rogues who lurked in the woods to rob travellers, and who even attacked farms and villages.

Savage punishments were dealt out to those who were caught, but it began to be realised that the poor must be given some help to keep them from crime.

The Poor Laws of Queen Elizabeth's reign punished the lazy rogues, and made it the duty of each Parish to look after its poor people.

At the workhouse poor men and women were given work

An Overseer had to provide the poor with food and shelter, and also with materials, such as woollen yarn, so that they could work and help to pay for their keep at the Workhouse. The children were cared for and taught a trade. The cost had to be met by the Poor Rate.

The Poor Rate was a kind of tax on well-to-do householders, and the more paupers there were, the more money people had to pay. Because of this, each parish did its best to prevent unemployed wanderers from staying in the town.

In St. Albans, in Hertfordshire, the constables had to search the town for strangers once a month. Any strangers who came to live in the town had to bring with them a letter, written by a trustworthy person, saying that they were honest and reliable. They also had to find someone in the town who would be responsible for their behaviour.

The parish constable turned away wanderers from the town

Strangers coming to St. Albans had to have a letter of introduction

TUDOR AND STUART PUNISHMENTS

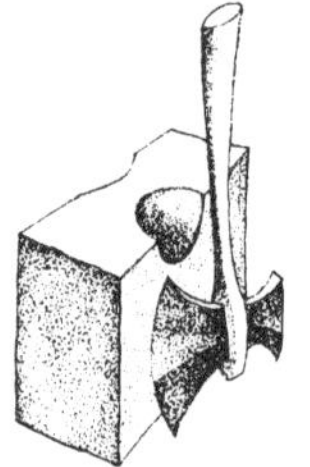

Punishments in Tudor times were harsh and cruel. Serious crimes such as murder, manslaughter, robbery and stealing were punished by hanging.

The severest punishment was for high treason. If a person plotted against the king he was sentenced by the judge 'to be drawn from the prison to the place of execution upon a hurdle or sled, there to be hanged until half-dead, and then to be taken down and quartered alive'.

People convicted of high treason were hanged, drawn and quartered

A noble who was convicted of high treason, although sentenced in the same way, was executed in a less shameful manner by having his head cut off. In this way, the Duke of Monmouth was executed for raising an army against James II.

The execution of the Duke of Monmouth

If a woman poisoned her husband, she was burned alive ; but a male poisoner was boiled to death in water or lead.

Perjury, that is, giving false evidence in court, was punished by the pillory, and by burning the letter ' P ' on the forehead. Rogues were pierced through the ears, and sheep-stealers had their hands cut off. Witches were either hanged or burned.

Witches were burnt at the stake

THE PARISH TAKES OVER

As the power of the barons and abbots declined, townsfolk and villagers gained a larger share in running their own affairs and in keeping law and order.

The parish was the important unit in local affairs. The parson and some of the more important parishioners met regularly in the church Vestry to conduct the business of the district.

By local custom, the inhabitants had the right to be called together at Easter, and at such other times as might be necessary, for this purpose. They were summoned to the Vestry by the tolling of the church bell. This was tolled for half an hour, and was known as the ' mote (moot) bell '.

At Bishop's Stortford, which was a large parish in Hertfordshire, the officers piously promised to ' meet at this parish church at the tolling of the bell upon the first Friday of every month for the settling the affairs and concerns of the parish '. If they failed to attend they were fined sixpence, a large sum in those days.

Villagers met in the church vestry to settle the affairs of the parish

The parish officers included the Churchwardens, who were in charge of parish affairs, the Overseers of the Poor, the Surveyor of Highways, who had to see to the mending of the roads, and the Constable. They were not paid for doing these jobs, and each year new officers were chosen, so that everyone should take his turn.

Sometimes the constable fixed his staff with the borough coat-of-arms to the door of his house

The Parish Constable was appointed at the Springtime Vestry Meeting. Anyone who refused to take the job could be put in the stocks and fined 6s. 8d.

THE MAYOR AND CORPORATION

Many royal charters were granted in Tudor and Stuart times allowing people to choose Corporations to run their towns. The leading citizen was the Mayor. He took charge at Council Meetings, and was also the chief magistrate of the town. So that he could have the powers to do this important job, the king made him a Justice of the Peace.

The mayor and the aldermen

In the Boroughs, that is, those towns which had royal charters, the Council chose the constables. When they were appointed, the Mayor handed each officer a staff. This was usually a short, stout stick made of hard wood. It was about 35 centimetres long, and was marked with the coat-of-arms of the borough.

This staff was the constable's badge of office. He had no uniform, and could prove his authority only by showing his staff. Sometimes he fixed it to the door of his house, so that people knew where to find him.

CONSTABLES

The job of Constable had never been a popular one, and when rich men were chosen they often tried to persuade the Council to excuse them.

Daniel Defoe, who wrote 'Robinson Crusoe', paid ten pounds in 1721 to be excused from parish duties in Stoke Newington, Middlesex. He said that it was a great hardship to force a man to become Constable. '. . . it takes up so much time,' he complained, 'that his own affairs are frequently totally neglected, too often to his ruin.'

If such people were forced to take the job, they would find some poor man and pay him a small sum to do it for them.

This was a bad thing, as the paid assistants, or deputies, were nearly always quite unsuitable for such a responsible duty. Very often they were old men, too weak to do an ordinary day's work! Such men were not able to stop fights and arrest dangerous thieves, and nobody had any respect for them.

The constable could call on anyone to help him

Bribing a poor man to take over the office of constable

One writer of the seventeenth century declared :

> 'I have known by my own experience that when hue and cry have been made even to the faces of some constables, they have said, "God restore your loss! I have other business at this time".'

At Dorchester a man was fined for calling the constables 'a company of dampened creatures', and at Exeter another had to pay for saying that the constables were 'overflowen with beer'.

However, many constables tried to do their work as well as they could. Sometimes they may have been harsh, but more often people blamed them for being too soft-hearted.

Flogging a criminal at the cart-tail

The constable could call on any townsman to give assistance in time of need, and people were in duty bound to help. There were many cases of men being taken to court for refusing.

Not only was the constable expected to investigate crimes and catch the wrongdoers, but he also had to carry out some of the punishments ordered by the justices.

The whipping of criminals ' from the waist up, till their backs be bloody ' was carried out by the constable. The offender's hands were tied by a rope to ' the tail of a cart ' and he was led through the town and whipped as he went.

The constable also had to duck scolds in the local pond, or force their heads into the ' bridle ', a fearsome iron gag. He had to set offenders in the stocks, and see to it that everyone in the market-place knew the full details of the offence. One woman at Northallerton was ordered to have a piece of paper set over her head, written on it ' in great letters ' : ' I sitt here in the stocks for beatinge my owne mother.'

A scold's bridle

Ducking a scold in the local pond

In the small country parish of Little Gaddesden, Hertfordshire, the accounts of the constables and other parish officers were kept in a stout oak chest in the church. The constable's accounts for 1675 include the following payments :

A parish chest where the accounts of the parish were kept

Pd. a man for repayring 2 bridges	8s. $5\frac{3}{4}$d.
for mending the gate at the Pound	11d.
pd. Rober Sim and Henry Tudor for guarding Rchd. Knight the first afternoone	1s. 0d.
pd. Rob. Segrave, Jho. Kingham and Will Gebroll and for candles to watch him at his owne house the first night	3s. 0d.
for passing a hue and cry for stolen horses	2d.
for making upp the Hedge and ditch at the field gate	1s. 4d.
given a poore man	6d.

The constable guards a prisoner

Stray animals were kept in the village pound

You can see from this that the constable had many different duties to carry out. Criminals like Richard Knight had to be kept safe, either in the constable's own house, or at their own, and guarded by villagers who had been called upon to help. It was also the duty of the parish constable to make sure that sheep and cattle did not stray. He had to see that fields were properly enclosed, and any straying animals had to be ' impounded ', that is, locked up in a special enclosure which was called the Pound.

Although the parish affairs were controlled by the Vestry, parish and town constables had to obey the orders of the Justices. They were expected to report to them at Quarter Sessions, and were fined if they failed to do so.

These reports were called 'presentments'. Here is the presentment made by the Constable of Little Gransden to the Cambridgeshire Quarter Sessions in September 1750:

Firstly . . . we have no common drunkards.
2. Our Hue & Cries have been pursued: watch and ward kept.
3. We have not been careless in taking up vagrants.
4. We have no unlicensed ale-houses or inns.
5. We have no unlawful weights and measures.
6. We have no newly-erected cottages or inmates.
7. We have no young persons idle out of service.
8. We have no market offenders.
9. Our highways are in sufficient repair.
10. Our town stock is used for the relief of the poor.
11. We have no profane swearers or cursers.
12. We have no riots, routs, or unlawful assemblies.

THOMAS DALE, CONSTABLE.

THE HIGH CONSTABLE

The Justices in Quarter Sessions once a year chose a reliable man to be the High Constable in each Hundred. In the country districts, the High Constable was usually a land-owner or a prosperous farmer. In the towns he would probably be a master tradesman or a well-to-do shopkeeper.

The High Constable reported bridges that were in bad repair

This job, like the parish constable's, was not very popular, particularly as the officer had to pay all his expenses out of his own pocket.

A Cheshire farmer wrote: 'I have made inquiries, and I find that a man cannot serve the office of High Constable without incurring a expense of not much less than £30 per annum.'

The High Constable had to report bridges that were in bad repair, check the weights and measures used by the traders in his Hundred, and give orders to the parish and town constables, or 'petty' constables as they were called.

THE WATCH

In the towns, watchmen were employed to assist the constables. Like the deputy constables, they were usually too old or lazy to earn a living in any other way. Their duty was to patrol the streets, to look out for wrongdoers, and to question anyone they found wandering about during the night.

A Watchman on his rounds

Shakespeare pokes fun at the Watch in one of his plays:

> Dogberry (the constable) : You are to bid any man stand, in the prince's name.
>
> Watchman : How if he will not stand ?
>
> Dogberry : Why then, take no notice of him, but let him go ; and presently call the rest of the Watch together, and thank God you are rid of the knave.

The 'Charlies' were often old men who were armed only with a pole

These feeble, broken-down old men patrolled the streets at night, 'armed only with a pole', said Henry Fielding, writing of them more than a century later, 'which some are scarce able to lift'. They also carried a lantern, and sometimes a bell. They did not wear any uniform, but dressed in thick, heavy clothing to keep out the cold night air.

These men were called 'Charlies', because King Charles II had said there was a need for them. Not until the middle of the nineteenth century did the Charlies finally disappear from the London streets.

4. LAWLESSNESS IN LONDON

By 1700, London was the home of one tenth of all the people in the Kingdom. With more than 650,000 inhabitants, it was by far the largest city in the land.

With so many thousands of people crowded together, the old ways of preventing crime did not work very well, so there was much disorder and lawlessness.

A street at night in 18th-century London

NIGHT-TIME DANGERS

There were mazes of narrow alleys between the main streets, where strangers could easily get lost. At night-time, with no proper street lighting, thieves and robbers could lurk in the shadows, in wait for likely victims.

Well-to-do citizens, going out at night, took armed servants and a ' link boy '

As far as possible, decent folk kept indoors during the hours of darkness. If they had to venture out, they went in parties, and well-to-do citizens took armed servants with them as a bodyguard, with a boy walking ahead of them with a flaming torch, called a ' link '.

Horace Walpole said that a visit to a friend's house for dinner was as dangerous as going to the relief of Gibraltar, 'owing to the large swarms of housebreakers, highwaymen and footpads . . . especially because of the savage barbarities of the two latter, who commit the most wanton cruelties'.

A footpad is arrested in Covent Garden

Householders had to barricade their doors and windows at night to keep out burglars. They went to bed with swords and pistols ready to hand, for it was a man's private business to guard his own house. It was said that 'every man's house is his castle, which he ought to defend'.

THE POOR PEOPLE

Thousands of Londoners, herded together in filthy slums, lived by thieving because they had no regular work. Droves of homeless children slept in the streets or in backyards, and as they had no one to look after them, they soon became the pupils of hardened criminals, who trained them to all sorts of wrongdoing, especially picking pockets.

The mob assemble to pull down a house

A young pickpocket at work

In the eighteenth century, gin-drinking became a serious evil. Gin, at first called 'Geneva', was a strong spirit which could be bought very cheaply. Poor people often made themselves drunk in an effort to forget their miseries. Not only grown-ups, but also children and babies-in-arms drank this dangerous liquor. Gin-sellers advertised that people could get drunk for a penny, dead drunk for twopence, with no charge for straw to lie on while they slept.

Gin-sodden men and women, hungry and ill, often committed crimes that they would have been ashamed of when sober. Conditions in London became a disgrace to a civilised nation, yet there was no organised force to restore decency.

'Gin Lane': this is an engraving by Hogarth, an eighteenth-century artist

THE LONDON MOB

Whenever there was any excitement, crowds of rowdy hooligans gathered in the streets, ready for mischief and violence. The parish constables and watchmen, armed only with their wooden staves, were quite unable to control an unruly mob, let alone bring the ringleaders to justice.

Wilkes' Riots: these riots were started by a Member of Parliament, who wrote a pamphlet against the king in 1763

During a riot, the mob was often joined by the apprentices. These lads, who lived with a master in order to learn a trade, worked long hours without pay. Some were ill-treated, and few had any opportunity for exercise or recreation. A riot was a fine excuse to down tools, grab cudgels, and rush out into the street to join in the general excitement.

An attack by Mohocks, young hooligans who roamed the streets

ROWDY LONDONERS

In the eighteenth century, at the time of Dean Swift and Addison, bands of well-born young hooligans, known as the 'Mohocks', roamed the town at night looking for mischief to do.

One person living at that time wrote: '. . . their way is to meet people in the streets and stop them, and begin to banter them, and if they make any answer, they lay on them with sticks, and toss them from one to another in a very rude manner'.

Unlike ordinary criminals, the Mohocks did not do these things for gain. It was senseless behaviour in a violent and drunken age. The timid Watch was powerless.

A highwayman holds up a coach

HIGHWAYMEN

Another menace to the law-abiding citizen was the highwayman. These were robbers on horseback.

Inn-keepers or their servants were often suspected of being in league with the 'gentlemen of the road'. They were able to pass on information about travellers' baggage, whether they were armed or not, and what route they intended to follow. In return, they would expect a share of the loot.

Horace Walpole said that some London highwaymen had grown so bold as to hold up coaches openly in St. James's in broad daylight. Nearby Piccadilly is spoken of as being 'quite unsafe after dark', and in 1748 the French mail was robbed in Pall Mall at 8.30 p.m.

In 1774, the Prime Minister, Lord North, was robbed by a highwayman in broad daylight in Piccadilly, and his servant was shot and wounded.

Highwaymen rob the Mail

'Captain' James McLean

The most famous highwaymen in the eighteenth century were Jack Sheppard, Captain McLean, Claude Duval and Dick Turpin. These 'heroes' and their fellow-rogues continued to thrive until the use of bank-notes, better roads and faster coaches and the good work of Fielding's Horse Patrol made the trade unprofitable.

London highwaymen even held up coaches in St. James's in broad daylight

EIGHTEENTH-CENTURY PUNISHMENTS

Sydney Cove, New South Wales, where the first penal settlement in Australia was established

Most of the people thought that the only way to deal with so much dangerous crime was to punish wrongdoers very severely. A crime for which a person could be put to death was called a 'capital' offence. By the end of the eighteenth century there were over two hundred capital crimes.

Capital crimes, or 'felonies', included murder, horse-stealing, sheep-stealing, making false coins, stealing from a shop anything worth 5s. or more, and stealing anything from a person's pockets. Criminals convicted of a felony were called felons.

Men, women and children over seven could be hanged for even small thefts, such as taking a handkerchief from somebody's pocket. One penniless young mother was hanged for stealing a piece of cloth from a draper's shop to wrap round her cold and hungry baby. Boys and girls under twelve were often executed for trifling crimes. In 1777 a servant girl of fourteen was sentenced to be burnt alive for hiding whitewashed farthings.

Convicts on board a ship bound for Australia

Judges and juries often refused to convict people for trifling offences that would lead them to the scaffold. Usually felons who escaped execution in this way were transported to the colonies in America, and, later, to New South Wales in Australia.

On the road to Tyburn : an engraving by Hogarth

Executions in those days took place in public, and on 'hanging days' vast crowds flocked to watch poor wretches being 'turned off'. Shopkeepers and tradesmen closed their businesses, as all their work-people took the day off to go and watch the hangings. Wealthy people paid high prices for seats in special stands, or at nearby windows which overlooked the gallows. Pick-pockets and other rogues went busily to work amidst the great crush round the scaffold.

Punishment in the pillory

In London, the place of execution was Tyburn, near the spot where Marble Arch stands today. The gallows was nicknamed 'Tyburn Tree', and was a large framework from which a number of criminals could be hanged at the same time.

The pillory was still a common, and often severe, form of punishment. The crowds pelted the offenders with stones and all sorts of filth. As late as 1810, a London newspaper told its readers that 'Viguers, the miscreant placed in the pillory in Cornhill, is at present blind in consequence of the pelting he received. He was so much bruised and lacerated that he is not expected to survive'.

REWARDS

The government thought that criminals could be brought to justice more easily if rewards were offered for their capture. Anyone, whether he was a parish constable or a private person, could claim these rewards. Some men who made their living in this way were called thief-takers, and were generally hated and despised.

A reward of £40 was offered for the arrest of a highwayman attacking a stage coach, £200 was given to anyone capturing a robber of the Mail, and as much as £300 if the attack was made within five miles of London. The reward for catching a sheep-stealer was £10, and £1 was paid for the arrest of an army deserter. Burglars and housebreakers were worth as much as highwaymen.

Such rewards certainly led to the capture of many criminals, but they also encouraged wicked people to lead youths into crime so that they could get the reward for betraying them.

In 1768 five men formed a partnership, and persuaded some foolish fellows to rob coaches. The partners informed the constables, the highwaymen were arrested, and the informers collected as much as £960 in rewards.

THE THIEF-TAKER GENERAL

The most notorious thief-taker of all time was Jonathan Wild. In 1708, he set up in business to get back stolen property for people who had been robbed. As he offered to return stolen goods for much less money than it would cost to replace them, his business thrived. People came to his office after they had been robbed, paid a fee of a crown, and had the details of their loss entered into a book by a clerk.

Thieves soon found that if they took their loot to Wild he would pay

A 'joke' invitation to Jonathan Wild's execution

them more than they could get anywhere else, so it was quite easy for him to return the goods to their rightful owners. Naturally, Wild made a good profit on these deals, but as robbers and robbed were both satisfied, nobody minded.

Robbers knew that if they tried to cheat Wild he would inform on them and get them hanged, so most of them took good care to keep in with him. In time, he had all the London gangs under his control. He divided the town up into districts, and arranged robberies as he pleased.

Wild made himself popular with law-abiding citizens by continuing to hand wanted criminals over to justice, but there were a few shrewd men who realised what a great rogue Wild really was.

At last he was arrested, tried and sentenced to death, and on the way to Tyburn was hooted and pelted by the mob.

Jonathan Wild's house in Drury Lane

Jonathan Wild is pelted by the mob on his way to Tyburn

TRADING JUSTICES

In London, as well as in the rest of the kingdom, the High Constable and parish constables were under the orders of the Justices of the Peace. In the capital, however, the work of the unpaid Justices was much harder, and the hours were long. It was also dangerous, for there was always the risk of gaol fever being brought into the court by the prisoners.

As the work was so unpleasant, most gentlemen would not become Justices in London. Instead, the job was taken by ignorant and greedy men who were only interested in what they could make out of it.

Such men not only made money by imposing fines, but they also took bribes from wrongdoers they should have prosecuted, and arrested innocent people and then made them pay to be set free. Their offices were called ' Justice Shops ', because there justice was bought and sold, and the magistrates became known as ' Trading Justices '.

The constables and watchmen, seeing their masters making money by wrongful means, thought that they might as well do likewise. Many of these officers were in the pay of criminal gangs, and even acted as lookouts for them. They also took bribes to release criminals they had arrested, instead of handing them over for trial. It was said by some constables that they would not arrest a man until he ' weighed £40 '. In other words, they encouraged young criminals to commit worse and worse crimes until their capture was worth a £40 reward.

A watchman accepts a bribe from a burglar

Sir Thomas de Veil

No wonder Horace Walpole said in 1742 that ' the greatest criminals in this town are the officers of justice '.

THE FIRST BOW STREET MAGISTRATE

In 1729 a retired army officer became Justice of the Peace for the County of Middlesex and the City of Westminster. His name was Thomas de Veil. He was a ' trading justice ' as corrupt as any other, and actually boasted that he made £1000 a year out of his position, but he was a stern and brave man as well. Using thief-takers and informers, he made a real attempt to put down crime.

He set up his office in his house in Bow Street, Covent Garden, and soon became the most important London magistrate. Not only did he try offenders, but he went out and about with his constables to investigate crimes and make arrests. He often went in danger of his life, and had some narrow escapes.

HENRY FIELDING

Shortly after Sir Thomas de Veil's death, a very remarkable man became London's chief magistrate. His name was Henry Fielding. As a boy, he was at Eton, and when he grew up he became a writer. Some of his plays, which poked fun at the Government, were banned, so Fielding studied and became a lawyer. A little later, in 1748, an old school friend got him the job of magistrate at Bow Street.

Henry Fielding made up his mind that he was not going to be a 'trading justice'. As the job was unpaid, apart from the fines, this meant that he would not be as well off as de Veil had been. He said that he 'reduced an income of £500 a year of the dirtiest money upon earth to little more than £300'. Out of this he had to pay his clerk, Joshua Brogden.

Fielding was not in very good health, but he was strong minded and courageous. Like de Veil, he was soon going round the town raiding trouble spots. It was clear to him that if crime was to be reduced, three things were necessary:

1. The general public must help him.
2. The police must be made stronger.
3. The causes of crime must be removed.

Firstly, Fielding put advertisements in the newspapers, asking people to help him :

> 'All persons who shall for the future suffer by robbers, burglars, etc., are desired immediately to bring or send the best description they can of such robbers, etc., with the time and place and circumstances of the fact, to Henry Fielding Esq., at his own house in Bow Street.'

This was quite a new idea, and people soon began supplying him with information.

When Fielding started, he found that one of his assistants was a very able man named Saunders Welch, a grocer who was also High Constable of Holborn. Welch and the magistrate became firm friends. The High Constable had under him eighty parish law officers, and he chose from this number six who were honest and willing. He trained these men in the proper duties of a constable, until they were efficient and reliable.

Saunders Welch, High Constable of Holborn

Welch told his men that quiet but firm reasoning was always better than the use of force. 'I advise never to strike,' he said, 'except it be absolutely in your own defence; but striking at all, if possible, should be avoided.'

MR. FIELDING'S PEOPLE

For the first time the robber gangs found themselves up against a real police force, which, although small, was well organised.

A Bow Street Runner

It was not long before the newspapers were reporting their success: 'Near forty highwaymen, street robbers, burglars, rogues, vagabonds and cheats have been committed within a week past by Justice Fielding.'

When the six constables reached the end of their year of office, Fielding and Welch persuaded them to stay on. As they had handed in their staves they had no lawful position as constables. In the eyes of the law they were just like any other private thief-takers. Fielding had no power to form a police force, so the little band, soon increased to seven, had to be kept secret.

However, it was well known that the magistrate employed such helpers, and they were spoken of as 'Mr. Fielding's People'.

Sir John Fielding

The name by which they are best remembered is 'Bow Street Runners'. This was never an official title, and the name did not come into use until about 1790.

The Runners never wore any uniform. They were plain-clothes detectives, as any sort of special clothing would have given them away to the criminals they were after.

As these Bow Street police officers worked long hours pursuing and capturing criminals, they had no time to earn their living in any other way. Henry Fielding had to pay them out of his own pocket.

Henry Fielding's motto for success against crime was 'Quick notice and sudden pursuit'. If people told him straightaway when crimes were committed, his Runners were instantly ready to hunt the robbers.

After three years' hard toil at Bow Street, Henry's health grew worse, and his half-brother, John, was appointed as a Justice of the Peace for Westminster to assist him. John had been blinded by an accident when he was nineteen, but in spite of this he became a very able magistrate.

Between them, working seven days a week, the two brothers greatly improved the state of the capital. In 1753 it was reported that 'instead of reading of murders and street robberies in the news almost every morning, there was, in the remaining part of November, and in all December, not only no such thing as murder, but not even a street robbery committed'.

Early in 1754 Henry's health became so bad that he took a sea voyage to Portugal, where, later in the year, he died. His blind brother took over as Chief Magistrate.

THE BLIND BEAK

John Fielding was thirty-three when he took charge at Bow Street, and he stayed there for twenty-six years. He wore a black silk bandage to hide his blank eyes, and in spite of his infirmity, he was feared by all the criminals in London's underworld.

Word went round that his hearing was so sharp that he could recognise 3000 thieves by their voices. Like most rumours, this was probably an exaggeration. Even so, the 'Blind Beak', as they called him, missed very little.

The Horse Patrol

The good work of the Bow Street Magistrate was not overlooked. In 1761 he was knighted, and became Sir John Fielding. Ever since, with only one exception, every Chief Magistrate at Bow Street has been knighted.

THE HORSE PATROL

Although the blind magistrate had done much to clean up the streets of London, travellers on the highroads were still in constant danger from highwaymen. Officers on foot, however bold and resolute, were no match for a desperate criminal mounted on a good horse.

A turnpike keeper blows his horn to summon the Horse Patrol

Sir John realised that it would be necessary to have a force of mounted men to patrol the main roads. Good horses cost money to buy and keep, but at last the money was found, and on 17th October 1763, the Bow Street Horse Patrol began its duties.

Eight men were appointed, most of them having had experience as constables. Almost immediately, two more men were added, so that all the main roads leading into London could be covered.

Travellers were asked to report robberies as soon as possible to the nearest turnpike keepers. These men were given horns which they could blow in order to summon the Horse Patrol.

The Horse Patrol was successful right away. In the first two weeks of its existence only two robberies were committed on the highways into London, and the tobymen were quickly arrested. After that, the highwaymen and footpads round London disappeared. An Oxford newspaper warned its readers that ' several gangs of thieves have lately left London to avoid Sir John Fielding's parties '.

Unfortunately, the Horse Patrol was too successful. The Government thought that the highway robbers had gone for good, and would not pay out any more money for the Patrol. Only eighteen months after it had begun, the Horse Patrol was disbanded. The highwaymen came back immediately.

' THE PUBLIC HUE AND CRY '

The blind magistrate thought it would be a good idea to send printed descriptions of wanted criminals to all other magistrates in the kingdom, and he asked them to send him information to put into his circulars.

These were sent out four times a year at first, and were called the *Quarterly Pursuit.* They became so popular that a weekly paper was also sent. In 1786 the name was changed to *The Public Hue and Cry.*

The first circular in 1772 contained

Criminals were often recognised from descriptions in the ' Quarterly Pursuit '

thirty-six descriptions. This was one of them :

> ' Benjamin Bird, a tall thin man, pale complexion, black hair tied, thick lips, the nail of his fore-finger of his right hand is remarkably clumsy, comes from Coventry and is charged with several forgeries, the last in Liverpool.'

Many criminals, fleeing from other parts of the country, and hoping to lose themselves amongst the London crowds, were astonished at being taken by keen-eyed runners as soon as they arrived.

Sir John Fielding died in 1780 at the age of fifty-nine. By hard work, courage, honesty and persistence, he had shown Londoners how to deal with crime. It was due to him that the word ' police ' came to mean a body of men who protect people's lives and property and keep the peace, although the actual word was not used officially until 1786.

THE GORDON RIOTS

As the 'Blind Beak' lay dying in his country house just outside London, the capital was in the grip of one of the worst terrors it has ever known.

Lord George Gordon, leader of the Gordon Riots. Thousands of people protested at the cancelling of some of the harsh laws against Roman Catholics. The riots showed how powerless was the small Bow Street Police Force, for troops had to be brought to London to restore order

The trouble had started because Parliament did away with some of the harsh laws against Roman Catholics. Led by a strange-minded man, Lord George Gordon, a crowd of 50,000 strong marched in protest to the Houses of Parliament to present a petition. But the cause of grievance was soon forgotten when the mob ran wild through the streets, smashing and burning as it went. By nightfall the town was in an uproar, and the rioting continued fast and furious for six days. Chapels, prisons, and hundreds of houses were burned to the ground. Gangs of rioters terrified ordinary peaceful folk by their violence.

The protest march of the Protestant Association to the Houses of Parliament. This led to the Gordon Riots

Soldiers were brought to London with orders to fire on the rioters if necessary

The Government found that the parish constables and the small Bow Street police force were powerless in the face of such numbers of dangerous people, and 12,000 soldiers were brought from all parts of the country, with orders to fire on the rioters if necessary.

Eventually the violence was brought to an end. At least 700 people were killed, and the damage done to property was too great to be counted. The magistrate's office at Bow Street had been wrecked, and all Sir John's papers and criminal records went up in smoke.

The six-day terror of the Gordon Riots made people see that they needed a much stronger force to keep order. Nobody had liked the use of soldiers, but on the other hand, they did not like the idea of a police force. Many were afraid that they would lose all their freedom.

King's Bench Prison set on fire by the mob

THE HOME OFFICE

In Parliament Pitt puts forward his plan for a London police force

The Government set up a new department called the Home Office, and the Home Secretary was made directly responsible to the King for upholding law and order, but he had no strong police force to help him. He could rely only on the magistrates, the parish constables, and the Bow Street Runners.

In 1785, the youthful Prime Minister, William Pitt, showed Parliament a plan to provide police for the whole London area, but it was so bitterly attacked that he had to drop the idea.

However, seven years later, Parliament passed an Act which improved the police arrangements in London.

Seven magistrates' offices were set up, each with three properly paid justices. There was to be a magistrate on duty at each office at all times of the day and night. Six paid police officers were to be stationed at each office.

The Bow Street Police Court in 1809

An outstanding magistrate then took charge of the Westminster Office at Queen Square. He was Patrick Colquhoun, a Scotsman who had been Lord Provost of Glasgow before coming to London.

By 1797 the Chief Bow Street Magistrate was Sir William Addington who increased the number of police at his office. In addition to the usual six runners, he started a foot patrol of sixty-eight men.

Patrick Colquhoun

This was known as the Bow Street Patrol. Like the runners, its members did not wear any kind of uniform. They patrolled the streets within five miles of Bow Street.

There were thirteen groups of four or five men, with a captain in charge. Eight of these groups patrolled the main roads out of London, and the other five patrolled all the streets of Westminster. They started their duties at dusk and went on until midnight.

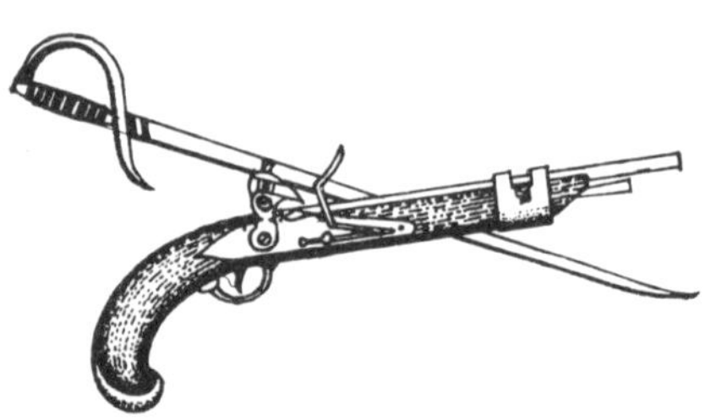

The men were armed with cutlasses, and the captains with a brace of pistols. The Bow Street Patrol were known to be efficient and fearless, and wicked men found that crime was much more difficult and dangerous. Even so, Colquhoun estimated that in 1799 there were 115,000 criminals living in London.

The Bow Street Patrol. Later, it became known as the Foot or Night Patrol

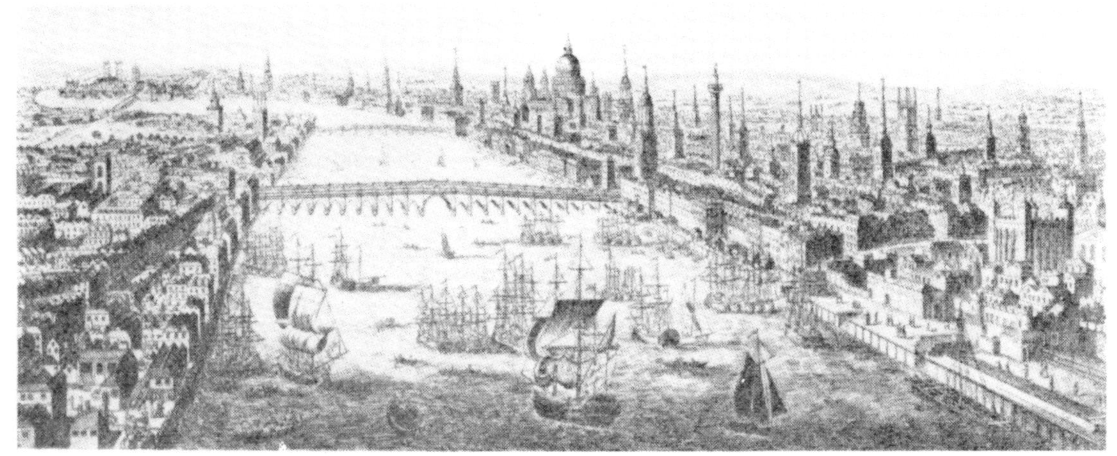

The Port of London in 1798

THE RIVER POLICE

The River Thames has been called 'London's longest street', and in Colquhoun's day this important highway was infested with smugglers and robbers of every description. Alongside the wharves lay many merchantmen laden with rich cargoes from all parts of the world.

Hundreds of similar ships were moored in mid-stream, and their merchandise was ferried ashore in lighters. Behind the wharves stood the great warehouses in which goods were stored when they had been unloaded.

Day after day, year after year, thieves took their pickings of the valuable goods which lay unguarded around them. Most of the robbers were watermen or wharf workers. There were also organised gangs, who would stop at nothing to get what they wanted.

Merchants and ship-owners were losing thousands of pounds' worth of goods every year, and when they saw the success of the Bow Street police in the streets ashore they looked for a similar remedy for the lawlessness on London's waterway.

Many robbers were watermen

A sea-captain named John Harriott went to the Chief Magistrate with a well-thought-out plan for policing the river.

Captain John Harriott, who planned the policing of the river

Colquhoun liked Captain Harriott and his plan. Between them, they worked hard to persuade the authorities to provide the money needed, and on 5th June 1798 the Marine Police was started.

A special magistrate's office was opened at Wapping New Stairs, right on the water's edge. Colquhoun was in charge, but Captain Harriott was made the Resident Magistrate, with eighty men to assist him.

There was a small fleet of well-armed barges manned by river constables ; Marine Police guards were stationed on the quays and in the lighters, and ship-constables acted as searchers on board ships unloading.

The Headquarters of the Marine Police was at Wapping New Stairs

The river police were threatened, abused and roughly handled by the gangsters on the ships and on the waterfronts. When the leaders discovered that the ' Ogglers ', as the new river police were nicknamed, could not be scared off by threats and violence, they tried to bribe them.

Captain Harriott dealt swiftly and boldly with all attempts to interfere with his men, who respected him for his honesty and firmness, and stayed loyal to him. Daily he was to be seen in his cutter patrolling the river himself.

It was not long before the battle with the river criminals was won, and the great port made safe for shipping.

The Bow Street Horse Patrol

'ROBIN REDBREASTS'

The Marine Police showed Londoners what a good police force could achieve, and its success persuaded the Home Secretary to increase the Bow Street police.

In 1805, the year of Nelson's victory at Trafalgar, he decided to bring back the Bow Street Horse Patrol. Fifty-four former cavalry troopers were sworn in as constables for Middlesex, Surrey, Kent and Essex. Under the charge of the Chief Metropolitan Magistrate, they were ordered to patrol all the main roads in an area roughly between five to twenty miles from Bow Street.

The men wore a blue double-breasted coat with yellow buttons, a scarlet waistcoat, a leather stock (a kind of stand-up collar), blue trousers, black riding boots with steel spurs, a black leather hat and white leather gloves.

They were also issued with equipment for their horses, a sabre and belt, a pair of handcuffs, a truncheon, a book of orders in a case and a pistol.

This body of men were the first policemen in England to wear uniform. Because of their conspicuous scarlet waistcoats, they soon became known as 'Robin Redbreasts'.

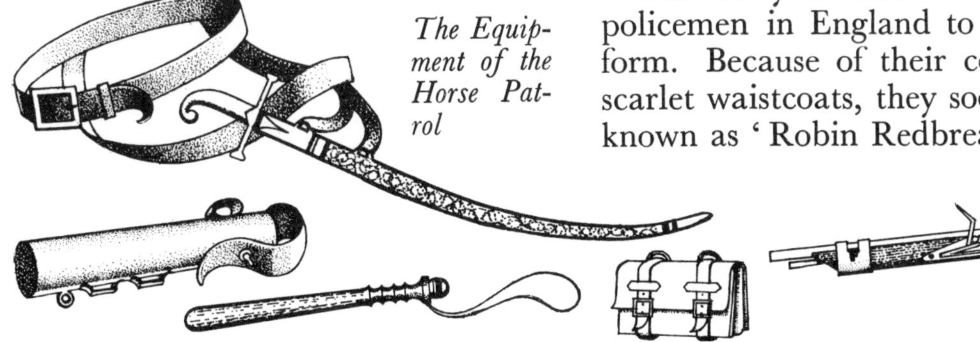

The Equipment of the Horse Patrol

Sir Robert Peel, who gave his name to London's 'bobbies'

The Horse Patrol was not intended to deal with crimes off the high road, such as burglary, and in 1821 a new force was formed to patrol the roads within five miles of Bow Street, on foot. This was given the odd name of Dismounted Horse Patrol.

There were 101 men, with a very similar uniform to the Mounted Patrol, but their equipment was simpler. As with the mounted men, their discipline was very strict.

In 1813 the control of the Horse Patrol passed from the Bow Street magistrate to the Home Office. A new Home Secretary was appointed in 1822, who had some very strong ideas about police. His name was Robert Peel.

Peel at once made several improvements. He appointed a Head Constable, or Inspector, to each of the seven magistrates' offices, which were by that time called Police Offices. A Daytime Patrol of twenty-seven men was started, who were to patrol the streets from 9 a.m. until 7 p.m., when the night parties took over. They wore the same uniforms as the Dismounted Horse Patrol.

The Daytime Patrol (or dismounted Horse Patrol)

HOW ENGLAND WAS POLICED

In the hundred years since Jonathan Wild had been executed, a great improvement had taken place in the policing of London. In the rest of England, things were much the same as they had been in 1725, although some of the large towns, such as Bristol, had well-run police systems.

A magistrate

The policing of England in 1825 was as follows :

A watchman

1. Throughout the Kingdom :

Justices of the Peace (unpaid)

Petty Constables and High Constables elected yearly (unpaid)

Paid Deputies

Watchmen, also paid

2. London (the Metropolis), as well as these, had the following paid officers :

A Bow Street Runner

Stipendiary (paid) magistrates, with the Chief Metropolitan Magistrate at Bow Street

Constables controlled by the magistrates

Bow Street Runners

Bow Street Patrol

Horse Patrol (Robin Redbreasts), Dismounted Horse Patrol, Daytime Patrol, all in uniform, and controlled by the Home Secretary.

A 'Robin Redbreast'

Thus the one and a quarter million people then living in London were policed by about three hundred men.

5. THE NEW POLICE

WANDERING BEGGARS

Although London was better policed during the first years of the nineteenth century than it ever had been, Robert Peel soon found that there was more work for the police to do. After the long wars against Napoleon, there were hundreds of out-of-work soldiers and sailors roaming about the country.

Many men roamed the country looking for work

There were also many other people tramping the highways in search of work, and most of these were attracted to the towns, where work could be found in the new mills and factories.

In the towns, where new machinery was being introduced, work could be found in mills and factories

MORE RIOTS

Much new machinery was being introduced, and workers were afraid that the machines would put them out of work. Such fears led to disorders and rioting.

Workers broke up the machines which they feared would take their place

One of the most serious riots occurred in Manchester in 1819. A protest meeting had been called in a public place called St. Peter's Fields. The local magistrates, fearing trouble, arranged for mounted soldiers to be on hand. Owing to a mistake, these Yeomanry were ordered to charge the peaceful crowd with their sabres drawn.

The 'Peterloo Massacre' (1819), when yeomanry charged a crowd of protesting workers

Panic spread like wildfire, and the crowd stampeded. Scores were hurt in the crush, some were trampled under the horses' hooves or were slashed by sabres. This unfortunate event became known as the 'Peterloo Massacre'.

Outside London, the authorities now realised the folly of using soldiers to keep the peace. But Parliament, magistrates, and local councils could not agree on a remedy.

THE METROPOLITAN POLICE

Robert Peel was convinced that the answer must be a strong police force under one command. Unfortunately, this idea was very unpopular. Many folk were afraid that they would lose all freedom if the police were controlled by the Government, and the Justices, the parish officers, and the City Aldermen were frightened of losing their powers.

It took Peel several years to convince Parliament that his idea was sound. When he was told that people were afraid of losing their freedom, he retorted, 'I want to teach them that liberty does not consist in having your house robbed by organised gangs of thieves'.

At last, in July 1829, Parliament passed the Metropolitan Police Act, and on the evening of Tuesday, 29th September, the first Metropolitan Policemen appeared in the streets. The word 'Metropolitan' means belonging to the Metropolis. Metropolis is a Greek word meaning 'mother city'.

The New Police wore a uniform, but Peel thought that it was most important that they should not look in the least like soldiers, so they were dressed as much like civilians as possible.

Each man was fitted with a dark blue tail coat with metal buttons, and dark blue trousers. The coat had a stand-up collar stiffened with leather, and on this was fixed the constable's number. He wore a wide leather belt, and a tall ' chimney-pot' hat which had a thick leather top and was stiffened at the sides with cane. Top hats were replaced by helmets in 1864.

The only weapon a policeman carried was a wooden truncheon, contained in a leather case hidden beneath the long tails of his coat. This staff was made of very hard wood, such as lignum vitae. In time, a looped leather strap was attached to the handle. This was to prevent the truncheon from being snatched out of the officer's grasp.

Every constable was issued with a rattle, to use when he needed help.

'Peelers' : the 'Peeler's' overcoat was covered by a cape in wet weather

Whistles were not thought to be as effective, but eventually they took the place of rattles during the 1860's.

During the hours of darkness the men were issued with an oil lantern, which was fitted with a round lens of glass, called a ' bull's-eye '.

In the summer, constables were allowed to wear light grey trousers. For winter wear they had a double-breasted brown overcoat, which had a cape to be buttoned on in wet weather.

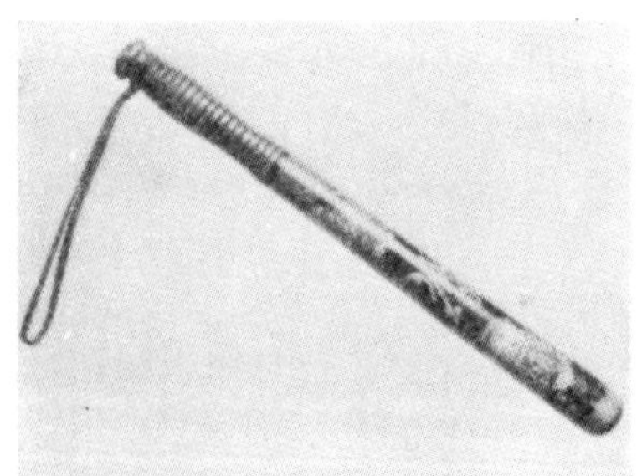

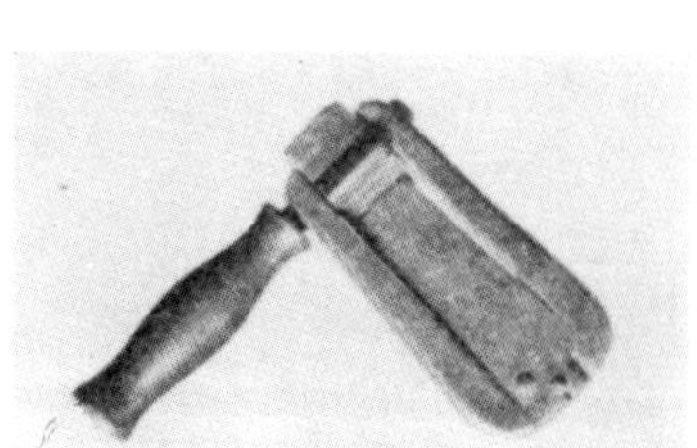

Every constable had a truncheon, a rattle and, during the hours of darkness, a lantern

Towards the end of 1829, a blue-and-white striped armlet was added to the uniform. As the New Police had to wear their uniforms at all times, the armlet was worn to show that a man was actually on duty.

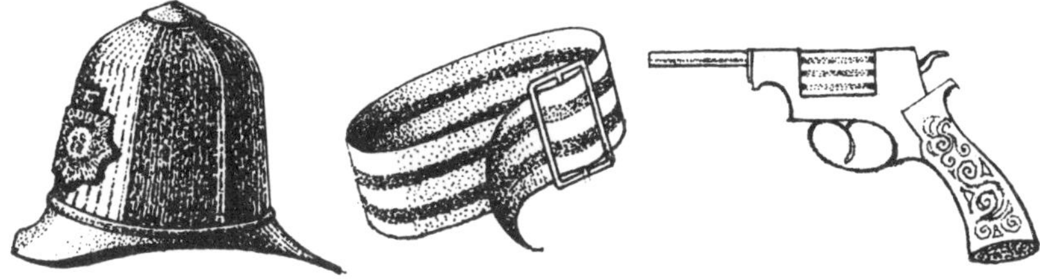

Each constable wore a helmet and an armlet; each inspector carried a pistol

Inspectors and superintendents had to buy their own uniforms. At the beginning, they wore no special badges of rank, but before long, ornamental braid was sewn on their collars.

In 1834 each inspector carried a pocket pistol, but no other officers carried fire-arms.

THE POLICE COMMISSIONERS

Robert Peel put two men in charge of the New Police. They were called Metropolitan Police Commissioners. One was Colonel Charles Rowan, a very experienced army officer who had commanded troops at the Battle of Waterloo. The other was a clever young lawyer named Richard Mayne.

To start with, their headquarters were at the Home Office, but they were soon transferred to a private house nearby, No. 4 Whitehall Place. The back of the building was turned into a Police Station, which was entered from an old court-yard.

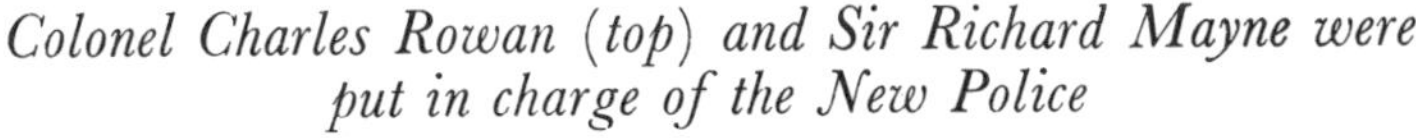

Colonel Charles Rowan (top) and Sir Richard Mayne were put in charge of the New Police

SCOTLAND YARD

In the days when Whitehall had been a royal palace, this yard contained a house owned by the kings of Scotland. Because of this, it became known as Scotland Yard.

Old Scotland Yard

It was not long before the headquarters of the New Police was referred to by the public as 'Scotland Yard'. To the men of the police force it was known as 'The Commissioners' Office'.

When a new headquarters was opened in 1890, further along Whitehall, it was named New Scotland Yard.

New Scotland Yard moved to its present address in Broadway, London, in 1967

THE ORGANISATION OF THE NEW POLICE

The Commissioners divided their force into seventeen Divisions. Each Division was named with a letter of the alphabet, and was in charge of a superintendent.

Under each superintendent there were four inspectors. Each inspector was assisted by four sergeants, and each sergeant was in charge of about nine constables.

The constables on duty each patrolled different sections of the Division. These sections were called ' beats '. The man was expected to walk his beat steadily for nine hours, at the rate of two and a half miles an hour. He was not allowed to sit down or lean against anything at any time during his duty.

All the constables were on night duty for two months out of every three, and they often had to attend court for many hours during the daytime.

THE METROPOLITAN POLICE FORCE, with the Number of Divisions, and the Population of each Division, 1830

Division	Superintendents	Inspectors	Sergeants	Constables	Total Police Force	Estimated Population
Whitehall	1	2	14	96	113	5,893
Westminster	1	4	18	145	168	51,618
St. James's	1	4	16	167	188	94,418
Marylebone	1	4	18	147	170	85,040
Holborn	1	4	16	147	168	73,208
Covent Garden	1	4	16	145	166	61,618
Finsbury	1	4	20	210	235	102,561
Whitechapel	1	4	18	168	191	111,382
Stepney	1	6	28	262	297	113,516
Lambeth	1	4	18	168	191	45,646
Southwark	1	4	16	168	189	78,169
Islington	1	4	24	222	251	74,455
Camberwell	1	4	19	195	219	64,967
Greenwich	1	4	20	182	207	72,540
Hampstead	1	4	22	190	217	70,260
Kensington	1	4	20	148	173	49,668
Wandsworth	1	4	20	146	171	57,532
Total	17	68	323	2,906	3,314	1,212,491

A constable on duty patrolled his section, called a ' beat ', for nine hours

It needed men who were healthy and strong to do this sort of work, and the Commissioners were very particular about whom they engaged.

A man who wanted to join the police force had to be under the age of thirty-five, and at least five feet seven inches tall. As well as being very fit and strong, he also needed to be able to read and write. In addition, he had to be recommended by someone in a trustworthy position who knew him well.

Men started as constables. A higher rank had to be worked for, and officers were only promoted if they had shown that they were fit for a more responsible post.

Rowan and Mayne angered many influential men by insisting that everyone who joined the New Police must start at the bottom. Robert Peel thoroughly agreed with the Commissioners about this. He said, 'I will not appoint gentlemen who would refuse to associate with other persons holding the same rank. . . . A sergeant of the Guards is a better man for my purpose than a captain of high military reputation'.

'The funeral of the city watch boxes.' This cartoon of the time shows how the New Police put the watchmen out of work

THE EARLY SUFFERINGS OF THE NEW POLICE

The 1200 men who first policed the London streets in September, 1829, soon discovered that they had taken on a tough and unpopular job.

Felons attack the New Police

Even the magistrates, their constables, and the Bow Street Runners distrusted the New Police.

The cost of the Metropolitan Police was met by increasing the parish rates, so many respectable citizens disliked them because it meant dipping more deeply into their purses.

It seemed as though everyone was against them. They expected to be hated by the swarms of criminals, but they were also disliked by the old parish constables and night-watchmen whom they put out of work, and by the parish officers and beadles who saw their power being taken away.

The titled landowners were afraid of being forced to obey the law more carefully than they had been in the habit of doing, and some of them encouraged their servants to resist policemen in the streets. His Lordship's coachman was egged on to lash them with his whip and to run them down.

Earl Waldegrave stirred up a prize-fighter called Young Dutch Sam to amuse the crowd in a Piccadilly tavern by beating up and nearly killing a policeman, William McKenzie.

On another occasion, 'Lord Waldegrave, Captain Duff and others committed a violent assault upon 224 Police Constable Charles Wheatley. A cab was driven over the Police Constable while they held him down, whereby he was rendered unfit for duty.' Wheatley lived, but was too badly maimed to continue as a police officer.

Earl Waldegrave paid a prize-fighter to attack a policeman

Insulting policemen became a popular sport, and many other brutal attacks were made on them.

In the courts a policeman who had arrested a wrongdoer had to conduct his own case, although he had had little education and only a slight knowledge of the law. He was usually alone, against a magistrate or judge and jury who disliked him, while the criminal might well be defended by able lawyers.

In court a policeman had to conduct his own case

Londoners shouted many names after the New Police, some more rude and unkind than others. 'Peel's Bloody Gang', 'Crushers', and 'Coppers', referred to the way they were supposed to treat people. They were called 'Raw Lobsters' and 'Bluebottles' because of their uniforms, and 'Peelers' and 'Bobbies' after Robert Peel.

THE SUCCESS OF THE NEW POLICE

The New Police were able to stand up to the hatred and violence which they met on every side, partly because of the devotion to duty shown every day by most of the men, and partly because of the fine leadership given to them by Colonel Rowan and Mr. Mayne.

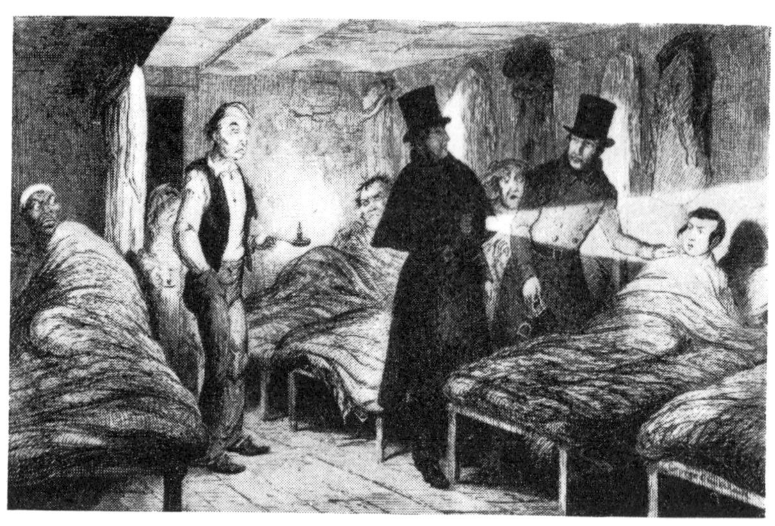

Constables in a lodging house arresting a felon

Like the Fieldings, Rowan and Mayne gave their men some wise rules. Each man, when he joined the Force, was given a small book entitled ‘ General Instructions for the Police ’.

The new constable read : ‘ It should be understood at the outset, that the principal object to be attained is *the prevention of crime.*’ The Commissioners went on to tell him that the protection of lives and property, and preserving the peace are also important duties of the police.

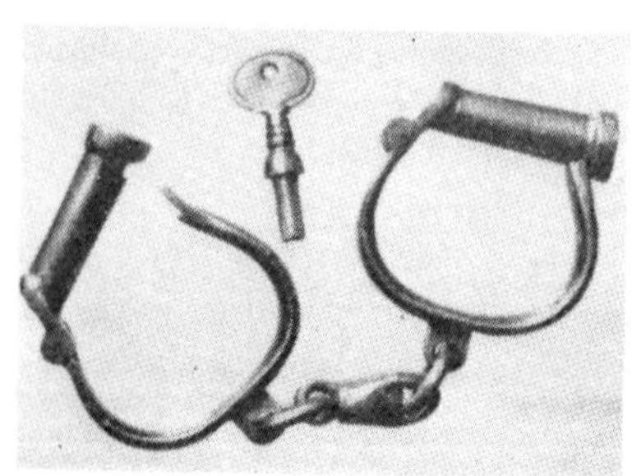

A pair of handcuffs

All constables were expected to control their tempers at all times. ‘ He must remember that there is no qualification more indispensable to a police officer than a perfect command of temper, never suffering himself to be moved in the slightest degree by any language or threats that may be used.’

By quietly carrying out the Commissioners’ rules of behaviour, the London policemen gradually persuaded the law-abiding public to look on them as friends and servants, not as bullies and tyrants.

The amount of crime rapidly grew less, and citizens began to realise that they no longer needed to carry swords and pistols to protect themselves.

THE NEW POLICE AND THE LONDON MOB

Unruly crowds tried to challenge the power of the police by attacking them

At the time when the New Police came into being, there were many people who wanted to change the Government. Some were prepared to use violence, and hoped to use the London Mob to help overthrow the King's Ministers. These reckless leaders made up their minds to challenge the power of the police.

In November 1830, a number of riots broke out, and the leaders of the mob gave out handbills telling people to defeat openly the New Police, and force the Government to disband them.

At first, when the unruly crowds appeared, the policemen simply lined both sides of the street and allowed the mob to attack them.

Then a tailor of Charing Cross, named Francis Place, suggested a new idea to Superintendent Joseph Thomas, who commanded the Westminster Division.

Place suggested that a strong body of police, with truncheons drawn, should be lined up to face an oncoming mob. When the order was given they were to charge the rioters and force them back with blows from their batons.

The first baton charge was made near Place's shop, and the surprised and bewildered mob were driven back down the Strand, through the gates of Temple Bar, and into the City, which the police were not allowed to enter.

For the first time, a mob had been defeated before any damage had been done, without calling out the troops, and without anyone being killed.

The police charged mobs with their truncheons

THE BATTLE OF COLDBATH FIELDS

The mob-leaders, seeing the success of the New Police, decided that once and for all they must be smashed. A ' show-down ' was planned for 13th May 1833.

On that day, a vast crowd assembled on an open space called Coldbath Fields. The Home Secretary had had secret information about the leaders' plans, and ordered the Commissioners to prevent the meeting taking place.

When the mob eventually gathered, they found they were surrounded by a large body of police, who had been hidden in nearby buildings. Colonel Rowan, mounted on a horse, was in command.

The angry crowd turned on the advancing policemen and attacked them with weapons they had brought for the purpose. Stones and brick-bats were thrown, and three constables were stabbed, one dying of his wounds. A baton charge was ordered, there was a short, sharp struggle, and five minutes later the mob was scattered.

The ' Battle of Coldbath Fields ' was a complete victory for the police. Although a policeman had been killed and several severely injured, there was not one person in the mob who had been seriously injured. At long last, the fearful power of the London Mob had been destroyed.

The two Commissioners worked side by side, building up their Force, for twenty-one years. Then in 1850, Colonel Rowan retired and was knighted by the Queen. Mr. Mayne was made a knight in the following year, and worked on single-handed at Scotland Yard, until he died in 1868. Since then the Metropolitan Police have always been commanded by a single Commissioner.

At the ' Battle of Coldbath Fields ' not one person in the mob was seriously injured

POLICE FORCES OUTSIDE LONDON

Criminals driven from London by the Metropolitan Police found crime easier in such large cities as Liverpool

The success of the Metropolitan Police drove large numbers of criminals away from London to other parts of the kingdom where a life of crime was easier. Citizens in these places began to notice the improvement in law and order in the capital, and to compare it with the state of affairs in their own towns.

In most places outside London, in 1830, the old parish constable system still operated. Although it worked well enough in country districts where there were few people, it was no use at all in the large towns.

Liverpool was already a great port, serving the new factory towns of Lancashire, and by 1834 its population numbered 240,000. There were only fifty watchmen to keep order amongst this huge number of people. It was little wonder that Liverpool was known as ‘ the black spot on the Mersey ’.

Portsmouth had 50,000 people, with twenty-two constables and watchmen. Hull, with 39,000 people, was one of the few towns to have a police force. The Chief Constable there commanded thirty-nine men, who were only paid when they made an arrest. Their motto was ‘ no prisoner, no pay ’.

BOROUGH POLICE

In 1835 a law was passed which changed the arrangements for governing towns. Each town, or borough, was to have a Mayor, Aldermen, and Burgesses. This group of men was to be called the Corporation. The Mayor was to be a Justice of the Peace, and chief magistrate, and the Corporation was to form a Watch Committee to appoint constables and provide a station-house.

More than a hundred corporations asked the Metropolitan Police Commissioners for help, and modelled their forces on the New Police. A number of London police officers became Chief Constables in borough forces.

COUNTY POLICE

The cost, time and trouble of bringing a criminal to court often discouraged ordinary folk from trying to secure justice in districts where the old-fashioned parish system existed.

In 1839 the Government gave permission to Justices in Quarter Sessions to raise and equip a paid police for the protection of the county.

Unfortunately, most of the Quarter Sessions did not bother to do anything. The first county to start a police force was Essex.

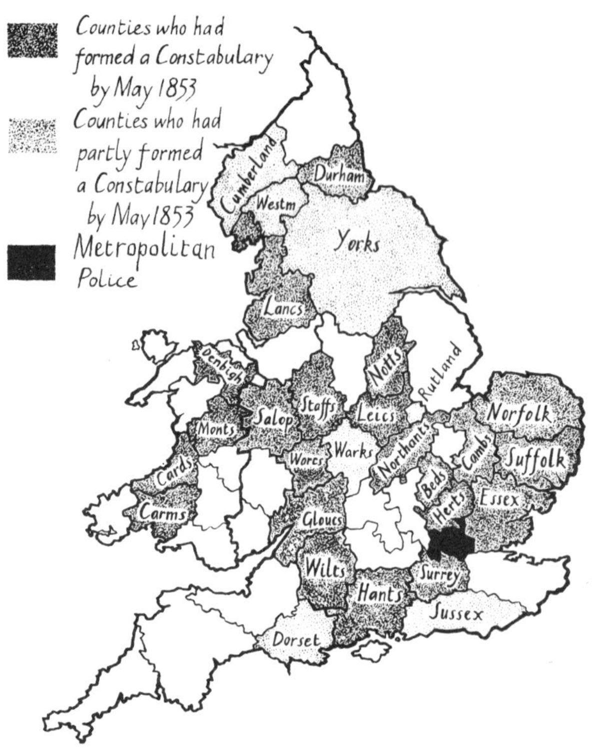

The County Police in 1853

The Chief Constable, Captain McHardy, made the Essex Constabulary so successful that the neighbouring counties of Hertford, Cambridge and Suffolk were obliged to follow suit.

By the middle of 1853, twenty-two counties in England and Wales had set up police forces, and seven others had made a start, but there were still twenty-two counties where the old parish system still carried on.

This was such an unsatisfactory state of affairs that in 1856 the Government made it compulsory for every county to have a police force.

To make sure that the law was obeyed, the Home Secretary appointed Inspectors of Constabulary. These officers were given the power to visit and inspect every county and borough police force. After each visit the inspectors had to make a report to the Home Secretary. If this report was satisfactory, the Government agreed to pay some of the cost of running the force.

In 1888 the Government placed the running of counties into the hands of County Councils, and the control of the police was taken over by a committee chosen year by year. Half the members were to be County Councillors, and the other half Justices of the Peace chosen by Quarter Sessions. This group of people was called the Standing Joint Committee.

6. THE POLICE TODAY

Helmet badge of the Metropolitan Police

A policeman of the City of London

The largest police force in England and Wales today is still the Metropolitan Police, with about 20,000 officers. There are 45 other forces, employing about 68,000 policemen and policewomen.

LOCAL FORCES

Although policemen all over the country are dressed very much alike, every force, apart from the Metropolitan Police and the City of London Police, is run by its own Local Authority Police Committee. Only the Metropolitan Police are controlled directly by the Government, and the Home Secretary is most careful to interfere as little as possible. The command of the force is entrusted to one man, the Commissioner of Police of the Metropolis.

The square mile of the City of London has its own police force, also commanded by a Commissioner. This force is controlled by the Lord Mayor and Common Council of the City.

Police forces outside London are commanded by Chief Constables, who are able men who have usually worked their way up from the rank of constable.

The Chief Constable of Devon and Cornwall Constabulary

A motor patrol constable

HOW ENGLAND IS POLICED TODAY

1. Metropolitan Police:

controlled by the Home Secretary; commanded by a Commissioner.

2. City of London Police:

controlled by the City's Common Council; commanded by a Commissioner.

3. County Borough Constabularies:

controlled by a Watch Committee; commanded by a Chief Constable.

Birmingham, Bradford, Bristol, Hull, and Leeds are the only towns which still have independent forces.

4. County Constabularies:

controlled by a Local Authority Police Committee; commanded by a Chief Constable.

Nearly all of England and Wales is now policed by big combined forces which look after two or more counties, or a pair of neighbouring large towns; for example, the Devon and Cornwall Constabulary, and the Manchester and Salford Police.

5. Other Police Forces:

controlled by public authorities such as the British Transport Authority, the Port of London Authority, the British Airports Authority and the Atomic Energy Authority; or by Government departments such as the Ministry of Defence and the Admiralty; commanded by Chiefs of Police.

THE C.I.D.

Every force has its own Criminal Investigation Department, and when a crime is committed it is the job of the local detectives to detect and catch the criminal. However serious a crime may be, it is not the concern of Scotland Yard unless it has been committed within the Metropolitan Police District, or unless a local Chief Constable invites them to help his officers.

This happens less frequently than when there were many small police forces. Nowadays, every force has a group of highly trained detectives who are experienced in dealing with murders and other such major crimes.

In most local forces a lot of difficult investigation is carried out by specially trained teams, such as the Fraud Squads and Drug Squads.

Detectives photograph tracks left by a vehicle at the scene of a crime

In recent years, in order to combat skilfully organised gangs who range beyond police boundaries, highly mobile squads of experienced detectives, known as Regional Crime Squads, have been set up to concentrate on the activities of these professional criminals. The Squads are commanded by a Regional Co-ordinator, who works closely with the heads of C.I.D.s of the forces in his area.

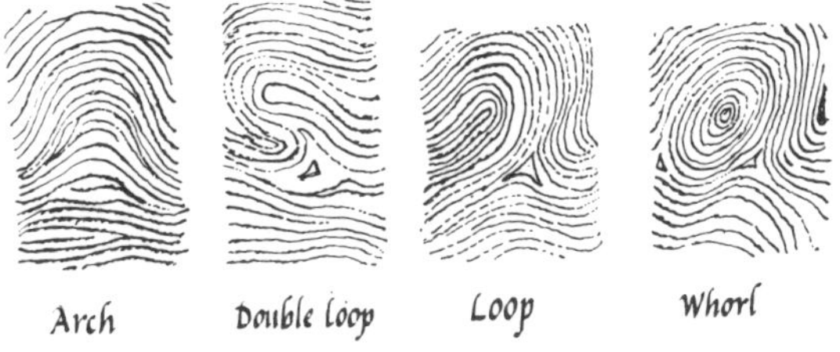

Different kinds of fingerprints

THE FINGERPRINT BRANCH

At their headquarters in New Scotland Yard the Metropolitan Police operate the world's largest library of fingerprints. The use of fingerprints for crime detection was brought to England in 1901 by Sir Edward Henry, when he was appointed Commissioner at Scotland Yard. It was while he was in India, as Inspector General of the Bengal Police, that he worked out a system for using fingerprints to identify people. He discovered the fact that every person's prints are different, and he thought out a reliable way of examining and comparing them.

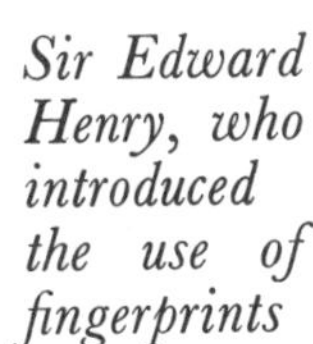

Sir Edward Henry, who introduced the use of fingerprints

Today, Scotland Yard's Fingerprint Branch houses millions of prints. Fingerprint impressions can be coded, transmitted by radio to Scotland Yard, identified, and the result radioed across the world in under two hours.

Searching through the fingerprint records

THE CRIMINAL RECORD OFFICES

The Criminal Record Office

At Scotland Yard there is the National Criminal Records Office which keeps records of all convicted criminals. It is commonly known to policemen as the C.R.O. The records include a personal description, photographs, the kinds of crime committed, when and where they took place, punishments, and the criminal's usual method of working. The huge collection of photographs is often referred to as the 'Rogues' Gallery'.

In order to meet local needs there are now eight or more regional C.R.O.s, and the officers in charge keep in close touch with the National Criminal Records Office. Preparations are going ahead for a national police computer to store and feed back all the collected information.

FORENSIC SCIENCE LABORATORIES

In various parts of the country there are special laboratories where scientists examine clues and carry out tests. They serve both the police and defence lawyers in the following ways:

1. They examine all sorts of clues, from dust in the turn-ups of a man's trousers to flakes of paint found on people and vehicles involved in road accidents. They test blood and hairs to discover if they are human or animal, and analyse the contents of a victim's stomach for poison.

Examining the plaster cast of a foot-print

2. They teach policemen what to look for, and what to do with clues found on the scene of a crime.

3. They are always searching and experimenting to find new scientific methods for detecting crime and bringing criminals to justice.

These laboratories are run by the Home Office, except for the Metropolitan Police Forensic Science Laboratory. When necessary, they can call upon the services of outside experts, such as chemists, dentists, doctors, gunsmiths, handwriting experts and other professional people who willingly use their skill and knowledge to help in the fight against crime.

WOMEN POLICE

The first policewomen were seen in London and Grantham during the First World War. At first, neither policemen nor the public liked the idea of women police, and it was many years before Chief Constables discovered what valuable help women could give.

In London during the 1920's women detectives were first used, but until the Second World War there was only a small number of policewomen employed in British police forces. Then from 1939 to 1945 women were used more and more and, by the time the war had ended, their usefulness was clear to everybody.

A policewoman in 1920

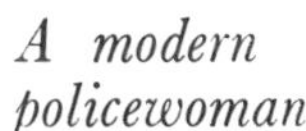

A modern policewoman

All police forces in England and Wales have a detachment of women constables. In 1968 there were about 3,000. The Metropolitan Police employed about 500.

A Metropolitan Police Cadet

The Commandant interviews a cadet

POLICE CADETS

Police forces recruit suitable school-leavers of both sexes as Police Cadets. They must be well educated and physically fit.

Cadets are paid whilst training, and wear a dark blue uniform which is similar to that of regular constables. On their shoulders is sewn a flash with the words 'Police Cadet' in pale blue thread. The head-bands of their caps are pale blue, too.

Cadets usually attend a local technical college for part of each week, where as well as general studies they study Law, Social Sciences and similar subjects. Tough adventure training, involving camping, climbing, caving and so on, helps to develop character, self-confidence, initiative, and powers of leadership. They take part in many sports, and are taught swimming, life-saving and self-defence.

A cadet learns to be of help to people who may be in need of special care and attention. Community Service is an important part of his training, and includes helping the aged, the homeless, and the handicapped, as well as youth work.

Towards the end of their training cadets are attached to various departments of the police force to gain some experience of practical police work.

SPECIAL CONSTABLES

Special Constables are ordinary citizens who volunteer to help the police at difficult times or on special occasions.

Members of the Special Constabulary are not paid for the duties they do, but they are given a uniform very similar to that of the regular police officers. The chief difference is that special constables never wear helmets, but always flat caps. When they are off duty they wear a neat blue and silver badge in the button-hole of their everyday clothes.

In 1968 there were about 35,000 'Specials' in England and Wales. They are given as much training as possible, and are called on to help direct traffic, control crowds or patrol the streets.

The button-hole badge and hat of a Special Constable

POLICE PROBLEMS TODAY

The New Police started mainly as crime-fighters, but it was not long before many other duties were given to them. Nowadays, apart from fighting crime, one of the chief tasks of the police is the control of traffic.

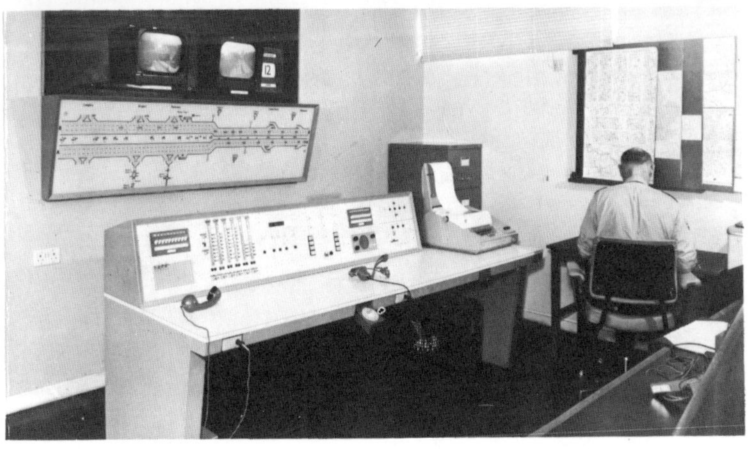

ABOVE
Police highway patrol at the scene of an accident

BELOW
A motorway traffic control room

Parliament has made many laws regulating the use of motor vehicles. Most of these are intended to make the roads as safe as possible for everybody, or to make sure that our ancient right to pass freely along the Queen's highway is not interfered with.

The police are also responsible for the control of explosives and firearms. They must see that the laws protecting children and animals are obeyed. Theatres, cinemas, dance halls and public houses are also the concern of the police, and so are many matters to do with public health.

Policemen are always ready to help anyone in difficulty

Foreign visitors can rely on the London policeman's knowledge of the capital

As he sets out on his daily round of duty the police constable has no idea what may be in store for him, or what serious and alarming situation he may have to deal with. Like the Boy Scout, he must 'be prepared' for anything that may happen. He will have no time to look for advice. The law and his knowledge of duty must be in his head. This is all he can rely on to do the right thing at the right time.

It is not often that you see a policeman running. He does not get excited. He acts calmly and steadily, and everyone can depend on him. His common sense, strictness, and sense of fair play have helped to create the greatest police force in the world.

TIME | CENTURIES | LAW | COURTS OF JUSTICE | JUDGES | LAW OFFICERS

British
500 A.D.
Saxon
1066
Norman
1200
Middle Ages
1500
Tudor & Stuart
1700
18th. Century
1800
19th. Century
1900
Present

Common Law (Folk Law)
Statute Law (King & Parliament)
Church Law
Petty Sessions ← Court Leet (local lord's court) ← Folk Moot
Hundred Court ← Hundred Moot
Quarter Sessions ← Shire Court ← Shire Moot
Assizes & Royal Courts of Justice ← King's Court
Church Courts
Magistrate's Courts
Royal Judges ← the King
Justices of the Peace ← Sheriff ← Shire Reeve
Magistrate ← Justices ← Lord's Reeve ← Village Headman ← Tribal Chief
Petty Constable ← Chief Pledge ← Tithingman
High Constable
Watchmen
Bow St. Officers
Police Forces

This summary shows how long some of our laws, courts, and law offices have lasted (e.g. magistrates' courts date from the early eighteenth century, and the office of Justice of the Peace has its origin in the Saxon Shire Reeve).

INDEX